Make It!

Making Games

Rebecca Sjonger

AV2

www.av2books.com

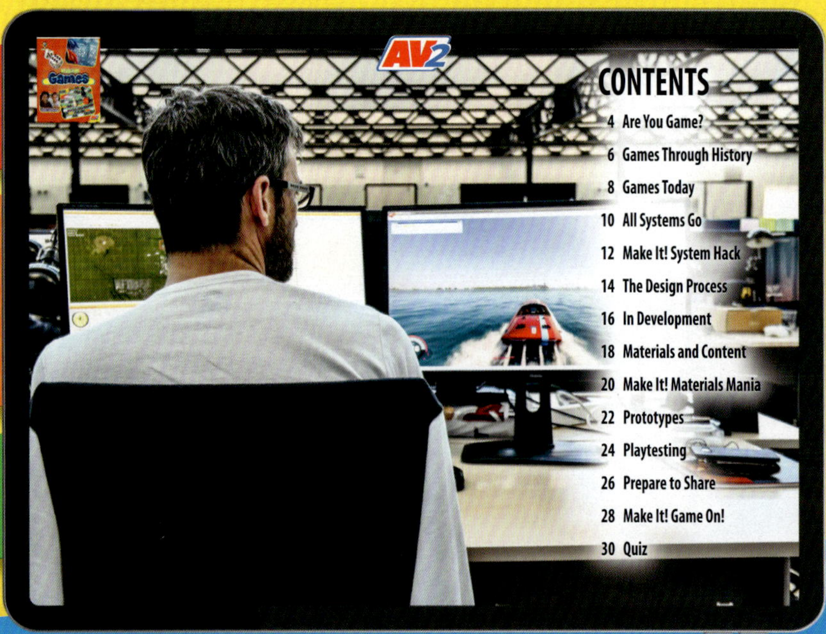

AV2
Games
CONTENTS
4 Are You Game?
6 Games Through History
8 Games Today
10 All Systems Go
12 Make It! System Hack
14 The Design Process
16 In Development
18 Materials and Content
20 Make It! Materials Mania
22 Prototypes
24 Playtesting
26 Prepare to Share
28 Make It! Game On!
30 Quiz

Making Games

CONTENTS

Are You Game?

Do you dream of constructing *Minecraft* worlds or have nightmares about crashing *Jenga* towers? Are you a fan of the *Candy Crush* game, or did you play the board game *Candyland* when you were young? Whether your favorite is charades, dodge ball, or chess, you belong to a huge group of people who love games.

Game Makers

You can do more than just play games. Anyone can become a game maker!

Nine-year-old Caine Monroy spent his summer vacation making games from cardboard. He built an entire arcade in his father's auto parts store in Los Angeles. Nirvan Mullick discovered Caine's arcade when he came into the store one day. Nirvan was Caine's first—and most important—paying customer.

Nirvan spread the word about Caine's arcade and its resourceful inventor. He organized a huge flash mob of new customers to surprise Caine. Nirvan filmed it and produced a documentary. The story of Caine's creativity and **entrepreneurship** traveled around the globe, inspiring other young game makers. This led to the creation of the Global Cardboard Challenge. Through it, more than 250,000 kids have made their own cardboard games and other inventions.

Maker Movement

Game making is part of the maker movement. Makers work in many fields, including animation, fashion design, and robotics. They find inspiration in just about anything. Makers take risks, are resourceful, and experiment hands-on with creative materials. Although their ideas sometimes flop, they can lead to greater inventions. In the face of failure, makers keep looking for innovative solutions. **Makerspaces** provide places for people to team up and share their tools and knowledge. Game makers often get help from other makers, such as graphic designers. Search for your local makerspace to get involved.

Skills Needed

Game makers are as diverse as their creations, but they each use many of the same skills. Math skills such as problem solving, reasoning, and working with data are valuable for planning games. Art and design skills are useful when creating game boards, pieces, and other graphic elements. Makers often **collaborate**, or work together, on projects. This way, each person can share his or her specific skill or talent to contribute to the finished project. The ability to work well in a team is very important in game making and other maker projects. Communication skills are central to teamwork and presenting your work. Developing these skills will help you win at making games!

Games Through History

Game makers build on a long history when they invent new games. Details about the earliest games are mostly unknown. However, ancient gamers left some clues. **Archaeologists** have discovered game pieces made from bones, shells, and sticks. Historical art depicts a variety of games. For example, ancient Egyptian images show a pastime called senet. It appears to be an early game of chance where players raced around a board.

Game Changers

Most ancient games have transformed over time. Mancala is one of the world's oldest **count-and-capture** games. It likely came from Africa and was spread by travelers to new places. In each new location, players changed the game's rules, the materials, and even its name. Hundreds of versions of mancala exist today.

*The length of a mancala board and the number of pits carved into the board is different depending on where the game was made.

Modern Games

The **Industrial Revolution** led to the mechanization of game making and new game-making technologies. In the 1840s, advances in color printing made publishing cards and board games more affordable. *Mansion of Happiness* was one of the first popular board games in the United States. It used a spinner to move players because dice were associated with illegal gambling at the time.

Electronic innovations led to an entirely new form of games in the following century. In 1958, American scientist William Higinbotham invented the first computer game. Hundreds of players lined up to play his game, *Tennis for Two*. Just over a decade later, video games were available to play in video arcades and on home consoles.

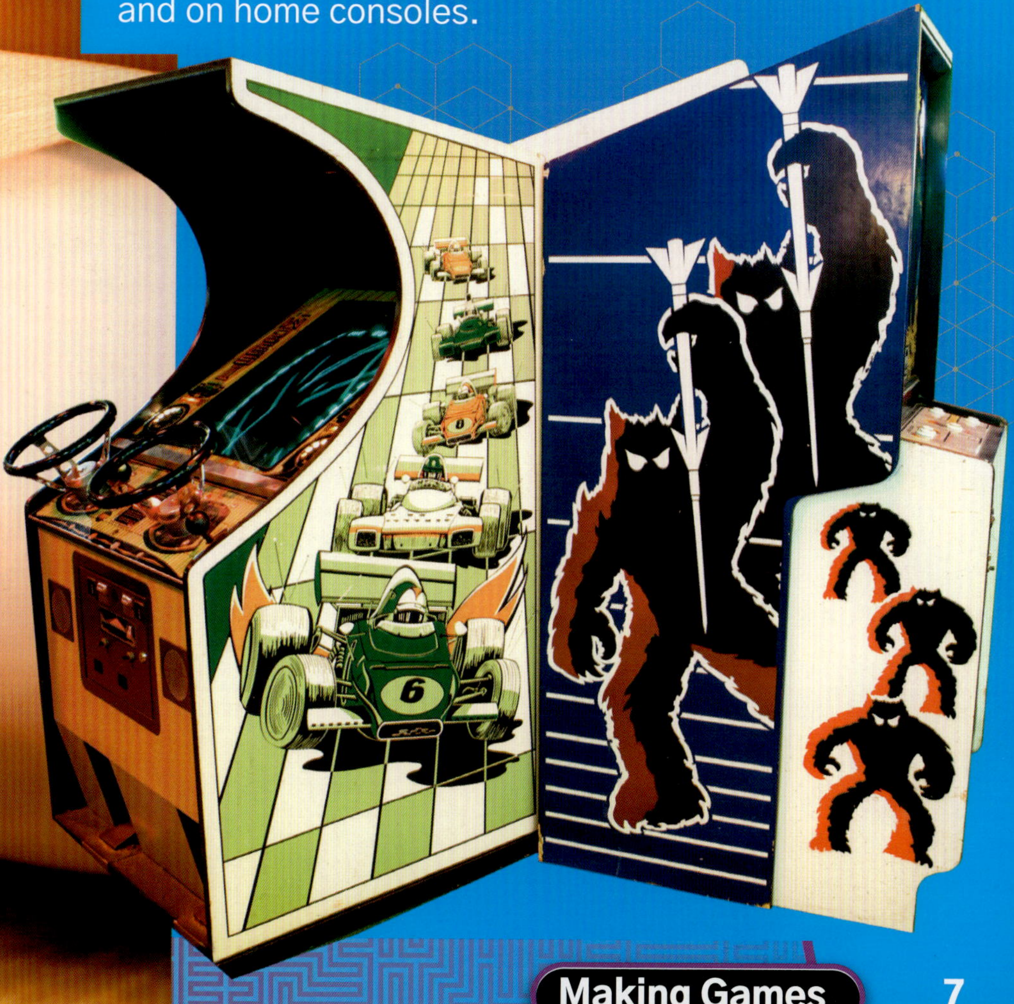

Games Today

What was the first game you remember playing? Chances are it was an activity such as hide-and-seek or follow the leader. After you learned to read, you may have started playing some of the games described below.

Tabletop Games

Some games are called tabletop games because we usually play them on—you guessed it—tables. Tabletop games are divided into four categories:

- Classic or family board games: These games, such as *Sorry!* and *The Game of Life*, depend mainly on luck.
- Strategy games: In these games, such as *Risk* and *Catan*, players must develop strategies or plans of action.
- Cooperative board games: These games, such as *Pandemic* and *Flash Point*, require players to work together instead of competing.
- Role-playing games: In these games, such as *Dungeons & Dragons* and *Tales of the Arabian Nights*, people become characters.

Tabletop games also include card games, such as *Go Fish*, and **deck-building games**, such as *Dominion*. In **collectible card games**, such as *Magic: The Gathering*, players trade cards to build their own decks.

Video Games

About one-third of the most played video games started out as board and card games. These games, such as *Scrabble* or chess, are redesigned for play on computers, gaming consoles, and mobile devices. The most popular video games are often action-based. Video game makers revamp and expand on old favorites. These video games series are called franchises.

Makers and Shakers

Elizabeth Magie and Charles Darrow

In 1903, Elizabeth Magie (1866–1948) made a board game called the *Landlord's Game*. It taught about **monopolies**, so players called it "the monopoly game." They shared handmade copies of the board and passed along verbal rules. Game pieces were small household objects. The game spread across the United States, and players in Atlantic City renamed the properties on the board. Charles Darrow (1889–1967) played this version with his friends. He made his own copy, called it *Monopoly*, and sold it to the game company Parker Brothers as his own invention in 1935. Darrow became the first-ever millionaire game designer. Neither he nor the game company ever gave Magie credit. She never profited from *Monopoly*, but eventually her role in making the world's best-selling board game became widely known.

All Systems Go

There are countless kinds of games, but they all have at least one thing in common. Every game is a system, or a set of parts and actions that connect together. A game system includes a purpose, rules, elements of strategy or chance, a game space, and game pieces.

"How To"

A clear purpose, or object, is the basis of a great game. For example, the object of *Clue* is to solve a murder mystery. Like all games, *Clue* has rules that players must follow. It is also important to know how a game ends. Often, someone wins a game by scoring a certain number of points. Other games end at a set time or when a player achieves a specific goal. *Clue* ends when a person identifies the murderer.

Player Engagement

A well-designed game system balances strategy and chance. *Clue* players can mislead opponents to improve their own odds of winning, but they have no way to control the roll of the dice. Game makers also plan how players interact with one another. In *Clue*, players can move an opponent's game piece by suggesting he or she is the murderer. There is an element of surprise—another part of the system—that comes from finding out if the other player was happy with the move.

Game Space and Pieces

The physical space where a game takes place is an essential part of many game systems. Its design may hint at a background story. The original space in *Clue* depicted the floor plan of the mansion where the murder took place. Later versions of *Clue* changed the spaces to go with new murder mystery stories.

Game pieces are also basic parts of the system. In *Clue*, plastic game pieces represent the players. Each color of game piece ties in with a suspect's name, such as red for Miss Scarlet. Rolling a pair of dice controls their movements. Each player gets a detective's pad and cards showing some of the clues. These pieces connect together to create a murder-mystery game system.

Make It!

System Hack

Find a game to **analyze**. Consider how its purpose, space, pieces, and instructions connect and work together as a complete system. Now you are ready to **hack** it! As a maker, to "hack" something means to change it in an extraordinary way.

You Will Need

- A game
- Notepaper and pen
- Objects for new game pieces (optional)
- The parts of one or more other games (optional)

Step 1

- **Brainstorm** as many ideas as you can for changes you can make to the game system. A few examples might include:
  Game board: make a new game board or use the existing one in a new, creative way.
  Game pieces: Add or take pieces away, or make new rules for using them.
  Game rules: Add or take away a time limit, or change how the game is won.

Step 2

- Review your list of ideas. Decide which part of the game system you want to try changing. Remember that makers take risks and are not afraid of failure.

Step 3

- Make the change you selected in step two—whether it is adding, removing, swapping, or rewriting. You will do a hands-on test of your work in the next step, so ensure your change is clear to other players.

Step 4

- Invite others to play the hacked game with you. If possible, play with people who are familiar with the original system. Ask for their feedback afterward, such as whether they could easily follow the rules, or whether the objective of the game was clear.

Conclusion

Reflect on your game playing experience. Review the comments from other players. How did the hacked system compare to the original system? Is there anything you would change if you did it again?

Make It Even Better!

Build on this activity by improving your hacked system. You could try a different idea from the first step. What do you think would happen if you made multiple changes to a game's system?

The Design Process

Makers each have their own methods for creating new games. Most game inventors follow an **iterative design process**, which is a repeating cycle of steps. Game makers may go back and repeat steps in the process as many times as they need.

Game design process

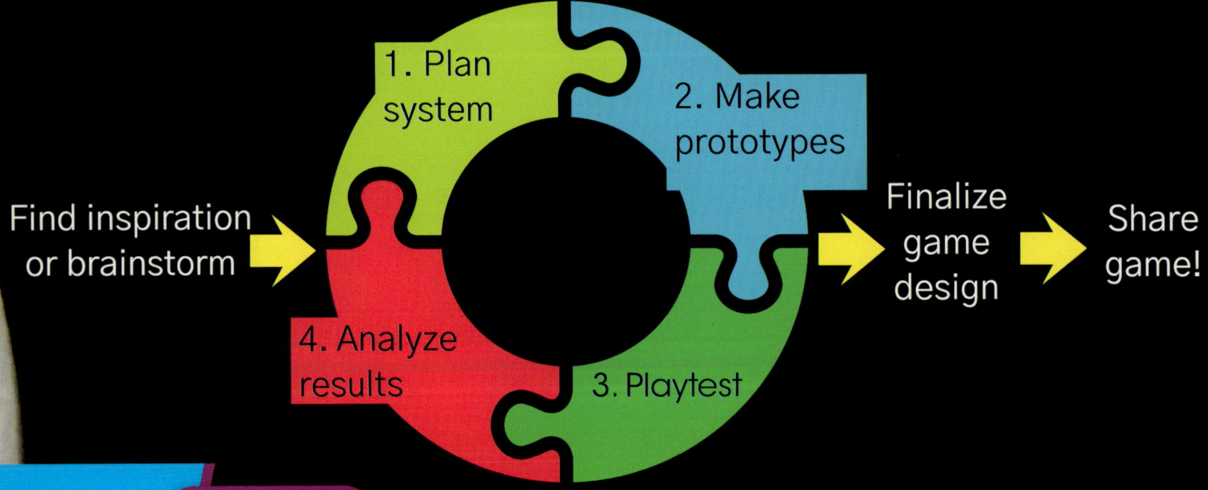

Getting Started

Makers kick off the game design process by coming up with an idea to develop—but where do they get their ideas? Inspiration comes from many places, including other games and brainstorming. Brainstorming is a timed group activity used to generate ideas. The next step is planning a game system. Makers write and draw ideas for each connected part. After the system is developed, it is time to make a **prototype** game. A prototype is a physical model used for testing. It includes all of the pieces and information that testers need to play the game.

Testing and Improving

Testers play the prototype during **playtesting**. This stage is vital for making a game that people enjoy playing. Makers analyze the feedback they receive and note which parts need to be improved. Then they return to the planning stage and refine the system. The cycle continues with a revised prototype and more playtesting. This is repeated until the maker is satisfied with the playtesting feedback. The last stage finalizes the design of the game. This may include graphic design, artwork, and written materials. They should coordinate with the game's theme. One last test run of the final product ensures that there are no glitches before it is shared widely.

*Most video games have a more complex design process than board games. Teams of up to 100 people work on designing them.

In Development

If you ask game makers where they get their ideas, you will likely get many different answers. Some people come up with game ideas that relate to their personal interests, such as hobbies or sports they enjoy. Other makers brainstorm to create long lists filled with new ideas. Later, they review the list and choose the best idea to develop.

What is the Point?

Once makers have an idea, they consider all the possibilities it presents. For example, if you love dogs and want to make a game about them, list everything you can think of that relates to dogs. Then, review your ideas to see if there is anything usable for the various parts of your system.

People need a reason to play a game. Choosing an objective sets the direction for planning the system. In a dog-themed game, players could earn points by answering questions about dogs. Or the goal could be to collect the most dog breeds in a card game. Can you think of other ideas?

Connecting the Parts

With an idea and objective in place, makers develop the rest of the system. They plan each part and ensure it connects to the whole game. To get yourself started, ask plenty of questions. For example:

- How many people will play together?
- Will they work in teams or compete against one another?
- What choices will they have or actions can they take?
- Will they face any obstacles?

Makers and Shakers

Richard Garfield

American Richard Garfield (born 1963) made his first game when he was 13. Since then, he has invented more than 20 different tabletop games. He was one of the first makers of collectible card games in which players build their own specialty decks. Later, he created the dice game *King of Tokyo* because he wanted a more interactive version of *Yahtzee*. Some of Garfield's other games came from more unusual sources. The inspiration for his card game *Pecking Order* was a "game" that he saw birds playing! His innovation has made him legendary among game designers.

Materials and Content

Tabletop games require game pieces. Games with time limits, such as *Perfection*, must include some sort of timer. Mah-jongg and other tile-based games obviously need tiles. Novice game makers can gain ideas and learn from game pieces used in existing games.

Game Pieces and Boards

In many games, game pieces represent players and are a good way to set a scene. In miniature war games, the pieces are very detailed and represent parts of the game's story. As a maker, ask yourself if and how the game pieces could tie in with the rest of your game. Game pieces can move in a variety of ways. Will you need dice, cards, a spinner, or tokens? Each of these tools use chance to decide where and how pieces will move.

Look at the designs of boards used in common games. A chessboard's layout allows for a huge number of strategic moves. In contrast, the fixed route in *Chutes and Ladders* shows all the pitfalls and rewards arrived at by luck in advance. Game makers must consider how a space balances strategy and chance.

It is in the cards

Games use cards in multiple ways. A 52-card deck is the basis for most card games. The numbers and suits on these cards mean different things depending on each game's rules. The cards in trivia games, such as *Trivial Pursuit*, and guessing games, such as *Taboo*, provide questions and answers. The purpose of other cards is to give players information they must use, such as in *Apples to Apples*. Makers of collectible and deck-building card games design each card to have a unique purpose, such as giving players special powers or rewards.

Make It!

Materials Mania

In this activity, you will design a simple game that uses objects found around your home. Remember, makers are creative and resourceful with materials!

You Will Need

- Any five household items of your choice. The following are some ideas to get you started:
- Coins
- Balloons
- Binder clips
- Buttons
- Paper clips
- Pencils
- String
- Toy horse or other creature

- Assemble five items found from around your home. You could include pieces from other games, as well as a mix of random things.
- When you have five items, begin brainstorming. Pick up each object and think of all the things it can do. Could one object form the game space? Would other objects work as game pieces?
- Write or draw as many ideas as possible. There is no such thing as a silly idea.

- Review your ideas and select the one that looks as if it will make the best game. Draft plans for a simple system.
- Is your game for single or multiple players?
- Which rules will make it harder—or easier?
- Are there elements of strategy and chance?
- How is a winner declared?
- Once you have mapped out each part of the game, make it!

Step 3

- If your game is for multiple players, ask friends or family members to test it with you.
- Play it several times and take notes describing the experience.

Step 4

- Refine your idea or try another one if the first concept does not work out as planned. Makers expect to make mistakes. They know that unsuccessful ideas are a valuable part of learning and improving.

Conclusion

Consider what you would do differently if you were starting again. Would you choose different materials? Would you use them in different ways? How can you apply what you learned about being creative with materials to the next game that you make?

Make It Even Better!

Did using just a few items make this activity more or less challenging? How do constraints limit or increase your creativity? Try building on your game or making a new one. This time, use any number of items that you choose.

Prototypes

A prototype game is a playable model. It is used to reveal issues with a system that the designer may not think of without hands-on experience, such as whether any parts are missing. Makers create prototypes for playtesting, but they may also solve problems during this stage.

Looks Do Not Matter

A prototype is a simple model that works well. Making it look amazing is a waste of resources at this stage. Game makers ignore how their prototypes look until the end of the design process. Instead, they focus on making the prototype playable with the right number of game pieces, rules that are easy to understand, and any other equipment that is necessary.

Many game makers piece together prototypes with inexpensive materials, such as sticky notes, index cards, and recycled paper. Different colors of paper or cardboard can stand in for different kinds of game pieces. Makers also borrow pieces from existing games. Adding a cheat sheet or materials guide helps players identify the different pieces and their purposes.

Clear Rules

Test players need all of the game's materials and content, even if they are in draft form. One part of the system that must be clear are the rules. Makers often create a computer file that is easy to update. You could also handwrite your rules. Remember to include:

- A list of supplies
- Set-up instructions
- The purpose of the game
- Rules for how to play, including how the game begins, how players move, and details about any obstacles
- Scoring information

*Playing a prototype allows testers to look for any flaws in its system.

Playtesting

Playtesting is a process in which a prototype game is played to see whether it works as expected. Makers often test their own games and notice parts they should improve. Try a solo playtest before testing it with other people. However, a thorough test needs multiple players and game plays.

Feedback

A game's first testers will probably be family members and friends of the makers. It may be helpful to explain to them what a prototype is and the purpose of playtesting. They should not expect to play a finished product. Ideally, the maker will not play with them, so he or she can observe and take notes. Makers often video-record playtesting, so they can review the sessions later. They try not to influence the game playing experience. When you are playtesting, avoid giving anyone advice or prompting them when they have trouble.

It is helpful to ask for more than just general comments after each playtest. Many makers prepare questionnaires with specific questions for testers. For example:

- How did they feel about the length of the game?
- What did they enjoy?
- What would they change?

Time to Refine

The next step is to analyze the game testers' comments. What do they see as the strengths and weaknesses of the individual parts of the game system? Once a maker has a list of changes, he or she incorporates the changes into the prototype. It is readied for another round of playtesting with either new playtesters or those you have already used. As you get closer to a finished game, expand your circle of testers. You need honest feedback from people who are not worried about hurting your feelings. The playtesting stage is complete when people say they enjoy playing it—and they look forward to playing it again!

Prepare to Share

When a prototype game is a hit with playtesters, it can move on to the final stage in the design process. Before sharing the game with the world, it needs to look great! You will also need to proofread the instructions and all other text.

Ready to Play

This is your time to shine if you are good at drawing or design. Makers may also collaborate with artists and graphic designers. Together, they ensure the look of each part of the game system matches the theme and feel of the game. They also make a box to hold all of the pieces.

The final game materials depend on what the maker plans to do with it. If you want one handmade copy, use durable materials such as bristol board and cardstock. Be creative with objects found around your home for game pieces. Game makers who want multiple copies may use game pieces and boards that can be easily produced by hand or printed from their computers.

Hello, World!

Most makers play their new games one last time when they are complete. You do not want new players to discover a glitch that slipped in at the end! Finally, the game is ready for sharing.

Some game makers make their games available to online gaming communities. They may also take their creations to share at game conventions. People who want to sell their games often send them to game publishers, just like writers who send their books to book publishers.

Makers and Shakers

Child of Light

The design process for video games usually involves a large group of people with different roles and skills. One team working at Ubisoft, a video game developer, went a step further with their collaboration. They invited Bastien Alexandre from Cirque du Soleil to consult on a new game. He provided ideas for scenes as well as his theatrical creativity. The Montreal-based team also hired Coeur de Pirate(born 1989), a local singer-songwriter. She composed the soundtrack for the game. Together with animators, **concept artists**, illustrators, designers, and programmers, they created *Child of Light*. This role-playing video game got as much praise for its beauty as it did for the fun it provided.

Make It!

Game On!

From brainstorming to playtesting, this book introduced you to everything you need to know to make your own board game. Are you ready? Game on!

You Will Need

- Large sheets of paper and pens for brainstorming and planning a system
- Prototype materials, such as sticky notes, index cards, paper in different colors, and cardboard
- Pieces borrowed from existing games (optional)
- Supplies such as markers, tape, and scissors (optional)
- Clear tape
- A flashlight

Step 1

- Plan each part of your board game's system. Look back through this book to brush up on the basic parts: game rules, boards, and pieces.
- Ensure each part of your game connects and works together.

Step 2

- Make a simple prototype game that includes everything testers will need to play it.
- Remember to use inexpensive materials in this stage. You can borrow pieces such as dice or timers from other games.
- Wait until the end of the design process to make your new board game look great.

Step 3

- Ask friends and family members to playtest your prototype.
- Collect their feedback, including general comments and questionnaire responses.
- Analyze the data.

Step 4

- Build on your second prototype by making the necessary improvements identified during playtesting.
- Continue the planning–prototyping–playtesting cycle until everyone agrees that your board game works well.

Conclusion

Once your board game is ready to share, complete the design process by finalizing the artwork. If you need help with the graphic design, what are some possible solutions? Could you ask someone for help, or simplify the design requirements?

Make It Even Better!

What would happen if you changed the object of your board game? Hack your own game and find out! Altering its objective will affect all the parts of the system. Keep trying new ideas, and enjoy your game making experience!

Test Your Knowledge

ONE
Who invented the game *King of Tokyo*?

TWO
What part of a prototype should game designers ignore?

THREE
Which repeating cycle of steps do most game inventors follow?

FOUR
What are game pieces typically used to represent?

FIVE
What does it mean for a maker to "hack" something?

SIX
What type of game is mancala?

SEVEN
How many cards are in the deck used as the basis for most card games?

EIGHT
Who invented the first computer game?

ANSWERS
1. Richard Garfield **2.** How it looks **3.** Iterative design process **4.** Players **5.** To change it in an extraordinary way **6.** Count-and-capture **7.** 52 **8.** William Higinbotham

Key Words

analyze: carefully examine

archaeologists: people who study ancient history by unearthing artifacts

brainstorm: to come up with as many ideas as possible

collaborate: to work together toward a common goal

collectible card games: games in which people trade specialty cards

concept artists: people who develop art and design concepts for games and media

count-and-capture games: games in which players use strategy instead of chance to collect points from their opponents

deck-building games: games during which people build and modify decks of cards

entrepreneurship: the act of developing and taking on the risks of a new business

hack: to rework an original object or idea into something new

Industrial Revolution: a time of significant growth and changes to industries in the 1700s and 1800s

iterative design process: a cycle of repeating steps in which prototypes are tested and refined

makerspaces: places where makers gather to innovate, share resources, and learn from one another

monopolies: situations in which a person or group of people have complete control

playtesting: trying out a prototype game with players who provide constructive feedback

prototype: a physical model built for testing designs

Index

Get the best of both worlds.

AV2 bridges the gap between print and digital.

The expandable resources toolbar enables quick access to content including **videos**, **audio**, **activities**, **weblinks**, **slideshows**, **quizzes**, and **key words**.

Animated videos make static images come alive.

Resource icons on each page help readers to further **explore key concepts**.

Published by AV2
276 5th Avenue
Suite 704 #917
New York, NY 10001
Website: www.av2books.com

Library of Congress Cataloging-in-Publication Data

Names: Sjonger, Rebecca, author.
Title: Making games / Rebecca Sjonger.
Description: New York, NY : AV2, [2021] | Series: Make it! | Includes index. | Audience: Ages 10-14. | Audience: Grades 4-6.
Identifiers: LCCN 2020001731 (print) | LCCN 2020001732 (ebook) | ISBN 9781791123482 (library binding) | ISBN 9781791123499 (paperback) | ISBN 9781791123505 | ISBN 9781791123512
Subjects: LCSH: Games--Design and construction--Juvenile literature.
Classification: LCC GV1230 .S56 2021 (print) | LCC GV1230 (ebook) | DDC 793--dc23
LC record available at https://lccn.loc.gov/2020001731
LC ebook record available at https://lccn.loc.gov/2020001732

Printed in Guangzhou, China
1 2 3 4 5 6 7 8 9 0 25 24 23 22 21

062021
101320

Art Director: Terry Paulhus Project Coordinator: John Willis

The publisher acknowledges Alamy, Getty Images, and Shutterstock as the primary image suppliers for this title.